COMPOSER SHOWCASE
HAL LEONARD
STUDENT PIANO LIBRARY

Play The Blues!

AN INTRODUCTION TO 12-BAR BLUES AND BLUES IMPROVISATION

BY LUANN CARMAN

T0053226

Edited by Sharon Stosur

ISBN 978-0-634-05437-2

HAL•LEONARD®
CORPORATION
7777 W. BLUEMOUND RD. P.O. BOX 13819 MILWAUKEE, WI 53213

Visit Hal Leonard Online at
www.halleonard.com

Contents

Preface

cinating musical style called the blues! This book will provide you with a great
:s style and songs, and also give you a taste for learning more about improvising
board.

h you how to "play the blues" by:

the 12-bar blues progression and showing you how to begin to improvise on a
)attern

.-bar blues concepts through fun, easy-to-play arrangements of favorite classic

your music-reading skills through pattern identification

) read syncopated rhythms confidently, a hallmark of the blues style

expressing a keen desire to learn blues and rock tunes, inspired me to write this
range blues songs for them, and found that the arrangements worked well with
:s of learners, particularly with students who were inclined to play by ear. In an
their interest, I assisted them with "by ear" playing, or taught them solos by rote.
orksheet for each song to encourage students to read, and to apply music theory
vere playing.

is the Blues?

irt **I** are important introductory exercises that should be completed at your lesson
the worksheets and blues songs in **Part II**.

Part II: Classic Blues Tunes and Worksheets

- The worksheets should be completed with your teacher at a lesson, prior to beginning practice on the song itself. The sheets will help you with pattern identification, fingering, hand position, and syncopated rhythms.
- Exercises that ask you to play or clap rhythms are especially important. Working on these exercises with your teacher during lessons will ensure greater confidence and success in your home practice.

The learning process: hear it, see it, play it...
- It's a good idea to start out by asking your teacher to play the song for you before you complete the worksheet. This will help get some of the rhythms and pitches into your ear, which is very important.
- If you are having trouble with any rhythm—counting it, but not hearing it or "feeling" it well— ask your teacher to play the rhythm for you and then with you, several times. There is much syncopation in the blues, so it will help greatly to hear the rhythms first, and then get the "feel" for them readily. Even so, always be certain to know how to count out the rhythms, too!

Part III: An Introduction to Improvising the Blues

Improvisation is *not* required to play the songs in **Part II** of this book. However, your interest in learning to improvise will be sparked by learning the great blues songs in **Part II**.

The exercises in **Part III** show you how to improvise the blues, step by step. You can work in this part of the book at the same time that you are learning to play the songs in **Part II**, or you can study this section after mastering the songs in **Part II**.

You should begin each lesson by playing through **Part III**, **Exercise 1** (*Black-Key Improvisation*) with your teacher. Perhaps your teacher could record the teacher accompaniment, so that you can practice this fun exercise at home. It is a wonderful confidence-builder for any aspiring blues pianist.

Have a great time exploring and playing the blues. Enjoy!

Luann Carman
California, 2004

PART 1:
What is the Blues?

The blues is a type of American popular music that originated in the early 1900s. The development of the blues can be traced back to work songs and spirituals sung during the time of slavery in the United States. The lyrics from these early years were very personal, talking mostly about hard times. Later, since the standard 12-bar blues chord progression began to be used for several different styles of music, the lyrics reflected that style. For example, 1950s blues lyrics are even silly at times, and Country Blues has lyrics that are similar to Country-Western song lyrics.

Blues Styles

When a musician is on a **gig**, or perhaps in a rehearsal, the leader of the band may call out a tune and say it is a "blues." Immediately the musicians think of the 12-bar blues form. Next they will need to know which style. Some of the many styles that use the blues form are:

Country	1960s Surf
Rock and Roll	Rock-a-Billy
Swing	1950s Pop Music
Funk	Jazz Blues
Traditional Blues Style	New Orleans Style

There are two other blues forms, the 8-bar blues and the 16-bar blues, but most blues tunes use the 12-bar blues. As you can see above, just about any style can be played over it. The characteristics of the **riffs**, rhythms, bass patterns, etc. will determine the style.

Three Common Blues Characteristics

A song in blues style generally contains three common characteristics. They are:

- the use of a standard 12-bar blues chord progression
- a repetitive bass pattern, or walking bass
- the specific forms of the melody and lyrics

Let's look more closely at these three common blues characteristics.

The 12-Bar Blues Progression

Many songs use a 12-bar blues progression. If you want to play the blues, you need to be familiar with this chord progression. In fact, it is a good idea to memorize this chord progression so that you will already know the chords when you begin to learn a new song.

The 12-bar blues progression uses the I, IV, and V chords in any key in a distinctive chord sequence over 12 measures. Thinking in chords (I, IV, V) makes playing in different keys much easier.

The examples below show a 12-bar blues progression in its basic harmonic formula, using chords built on the first (I), fourth (IV), and fifth (V) degrees of the scale.

You can see from this diagram that the chord progression is I–IV–I–V–IV–I, moving over 12 measures, or 12 bars, hence the name "the 12-bar blues."

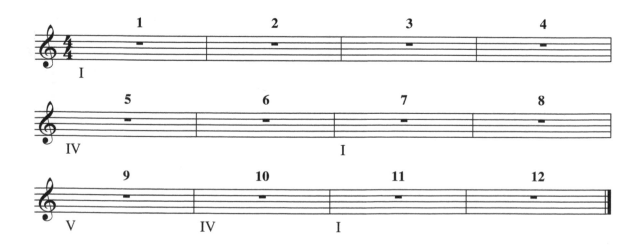

Here's an example of the 12-bar blues progression in the key of C. Note how the chord symbols above the staff lines correspond directly to the scale-degree symbols below the staff lines. (C = I, F = IV, G = V).

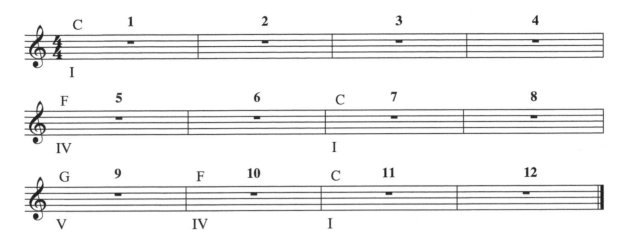

Please note: The chords of the basic blues progression (I–IV–I–V–IV–I) are actually 7th chords (major triad + minor 7th). The flat-7th adds to the bluesy quality and is always implied. Notation is loosely held in the blues and is often a matter of the writer's personal preference. For example, an arranger may choose to indicate F7, whereas another may choose F for the same measure. For the sake of simplicity, some of the earlier exercises and tunes in this book indicate only a triad and leave out the 7th. As your study of the blues progresses, you will see many chord variations to this basic progression, which include other chord qualities (minor 7ths, diminished 7ths, etc.).

EXERCISE 1: Writing Out a 12-Bar Blues Progression

Write the 12-bar blues progression in the key of G, using chord symbols (G, C, D) in the blanks above the staff lines.

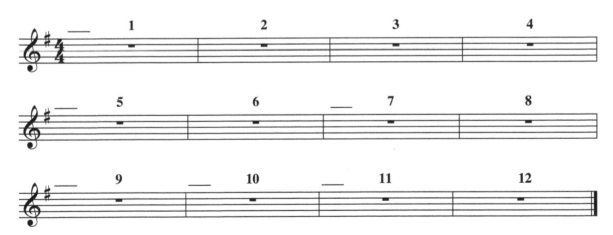

Now write the same progression in the key of D, using chord symbols in the blanks above the staff lines.

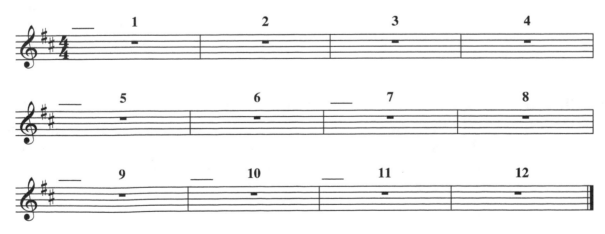

EXERCISE 2: Getting the 12-Bar Blues Progression Under Your Fingers

Now it's time to play the 12-bar blues progression. The following exercises are designed to get this chord progression in your ears and under your fingers. Play each one many times, until you notice that your ear takes over and you no longer need to think about the chord changes.

First, learn to play the basic 12-bar blues progression in the key of C.

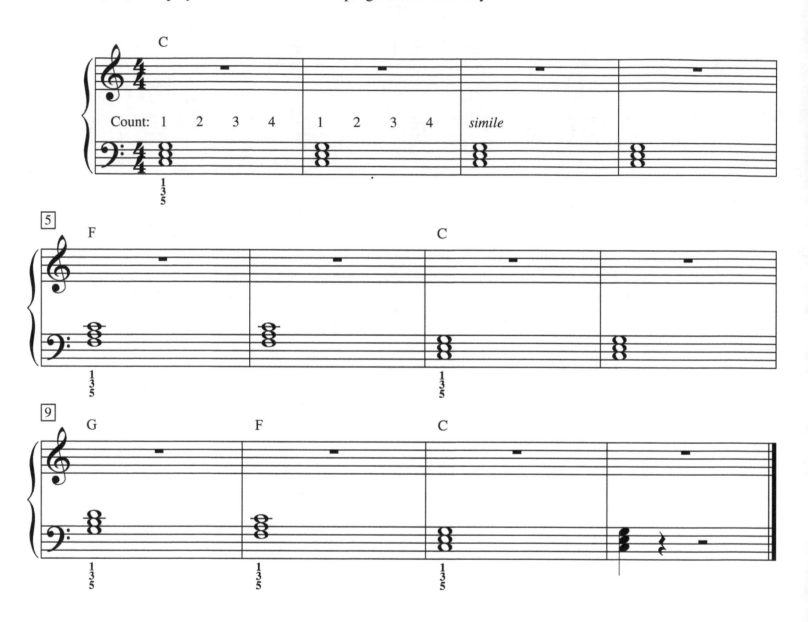

After you have mastered Exercise 2, memorize it!

> To **transpose** is to play a song in a different key than the one in which it is written.

EXERCISE 3: Transposing the Progression to Other Keys

Transpose the basic 12-bar blues pattern to the keys of G, D, and F. Ask your teacher to help you identify the chords you will use. Do not write them out. Use your ear to help you hear when the chord changes need to be made. Your transpositions will sound the same as the original exercise in the key of C if you follow the formula exactly.

EXERCISE 4: Moving Around the Keyboard Within the 12-Bar Blues Progression

Learn this simple exercise and then memorize it.

Blocked-Chord Blues

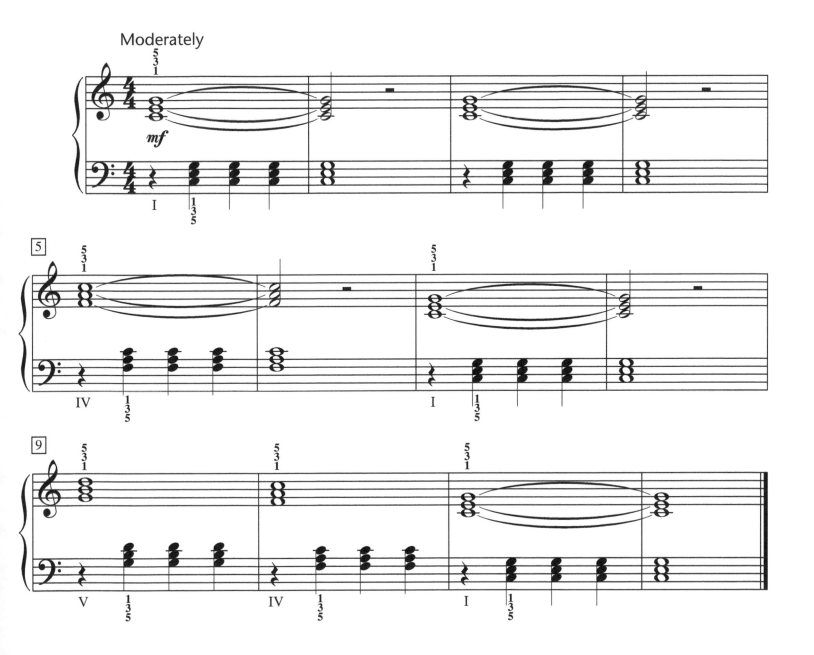

Extra for Experts: Transpose *Blocked-Chord Blues* to the keys of G, F, and D.

The Repetitive Bass Pattern, or "Walking Bass"

There are many bass patterns in the blues. These patterns repeat several times within a 12-bar blues progression, making the left hand predictable and easier to learn. The following **walking-bass pattern** is one that is common to several styles of the blues.

A **walking-bass pattern** is a bass line of steady quarter-notes or eighth-notes, usually moving stepwise and chordally.

EXERCISE 5: Walkin'-Bass Blues Warm-Up and Solo

Left Hand Warm-Up

Play the following walking-bass pattern. Follow the fingering exactly.

Now play the same pattern, starting on F.

Measures 9, 10, and 11 use only half of this pattern, starting on G, F, and then C.

Add your right-hand chords and you've got your first solo in blues style!

Walkin'-Bass Blues

When you feel comfortable playing through this solo and can play it with ease, transpose *Walkin'-Bass Blues* to the keys of G, F, and D. Practice, practice, practice!

EXERCISE 6: Walk the Bass, Get the Right Hand Movin'!

This solo has the same left-hand walking-bass pattern you just learned in Exercise 5. The right hand also plays the same chords as in Exercise 5, but on the offbeats. My students always have a lot of fun playing this.

Spencer's Groove

* This piece can be played with **straight eighths** or **swing eighths**.
  (See page 15 for an explanation of these terms.)

The Forms of Blues Lyrics and Blues Melodies

Blues lyrics and blues melodies are usually very simple. Their phrases follow similar structural patterns, or forms.

Lyrics

Let's look at the lyrics to *Bumblebee Blues*, page 19.

> *I'm as happy as can be, 'cause now you're my honeybee.*
> *I'm as happy as can be, 'cause now you're my honeybee.*
> *Sweet nectar's mine and I'm buzzin' like a bumblebee.*

In traditional blues style, the lyrics follow a specific phrase structure. There are *three* lyric lines that generally have this pattern:

First phrase: an introductory lyric line

Second phrase: repeats the first line

Third phrase: the rhythmic word pattern changes, and the new lyrics complete the thought

EXERCISE 7: Analyzing Lyrics: Hound Dog

Write in the lyrics for *Hound Dog* (page 23) below.

First phrase (pick-up through measure 3):

_____

Second phrase (pick-up, measures 4–7):

_____

Third phrase (pick-up, measures 8 to the end):

_____

Notice how these lyrics exhibit the same phrase structure outlined above. The first two lines are identical, with identical rhythmic word patterns. The third line has completely new words, completes the thought, and changes its rhythmic word pattern.

Melodies

Blues melodies, like blues lyrics, have *three* distinct phrases, each four measures long:

First phrase (measures 1–4): is played over the I chord.

Second phrase (measures 5–8): often repeats the first phrase. Even though the melody here may be identical to the first phrase, the harmony changes to the IV chord, giving the phrase a different sound.

Third phrase (measures 9–12): completes the musical sentence, and sounds like an ending to the first two phrases. The harmonic progression leads from the V chord to the IV chord, finally ending on the I chord.

There is a pick-up (see page 18) to measures 1, 5, and 9, offsetting the actual measures for the 4-bar phrases. Notice that this occurs in *Hound Dog*, on the following page.

A **riff** is a short melodic idea which has a particular stylistic sound to it; for example, blues, country, or jazz style.

EXERCISE 8: Analyzing Musical Phrases: *Hound Dog*

Write in the melodic phrases for *Hound Dog* below.

First phrase (pick-up – measure 3)

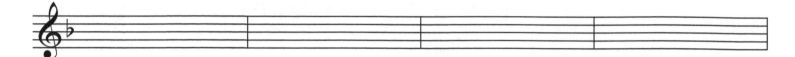

Second phrase (pick-up – measures 4–7)

Third phrase (pick-up – measures 8 to the end)

The Riff

Instead of the four-bar phrases we just studied, some blues melodies repeat a short and simple **riff** over and over. The melody in these pieces is a simple, repeated riff, usually every two measures, as in *Tutti Frutti* (page 29).

Write the two-bar riff melody found in *Tutti Frutti:*

Riff-playing became popular in the swing era of the 1940s and continued with rock music in the 1950s (as in *Tutti Frutti,* right?). The Count Basie Big Band used this device often. Using a riff as the basis for a tune made it easy for a band with a large number of musicians to improvise and eliminated the need for extensive arranging and charts for every player. The leader could play a riff and specify "C blues," for example, and they'd be off and running. *In the Mood; Shake, Rattle And Roll;* and *Jump, Jive An' Wail* are three other tunes in this book that use this alternate melodic form.

Straight Eighths, Swing Eighths

In any style of music, eighth notes will either "swing" or be played "straight." They look the same, but sound different. Clap all of the examples below and experience the difference for yourself. It is very important to have the right "feel," meaning the right rhythm.

Straight Eighths: eighth notes played as written, giving each eighth note equal value.

Straight eighths are often used in rock blues tunes such as *Jailhouse Rock* (page 27) and *I Got You (I Feel Good)* (page 35).

Swing Eighths: eighth-note pairs written as even eighths, but played as a triplet figure. Playing swing eighths is also sometimes referred to as playing a **shuffle rhythm**.

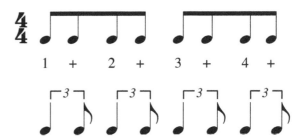

long short, long short, long short, long short

The eighth notes are written 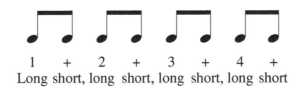.

It's a good idea to practice the swing-eighth rhythm by clapping it first. Clap and count the swing eighths below.

But how do you know when to play "straight" or "swing" style if the eighth notes look exactly the same? Usually, the arranger or composer will indicate "swing eighths" at the beginning of each tune, just after the tempo indication. In this book, I've indicated "straight eighths" or "swing eighths" for each tune so that there's no question which to play:

The tunes in this book that use **swing eighths**, or **shuffle rhythm**, are: *Bumblebee Blues; Shake, Rattle And Roll; Hound Dog; Blue Suede Shoes; Tutti Frutti; In The Mood; Jump, Jive An' Wail;* and *Night Train*.

PART II:
Classic Blues Tunes and Worksheets

Bumblebee Blues Worksheet

Write in the chord symbols for C blues in the boxes below:

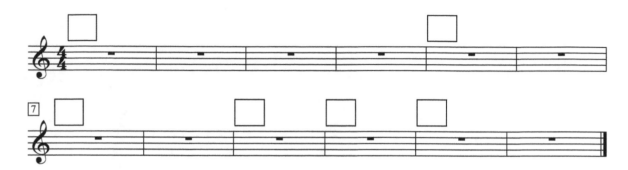

Is the beginning of *Bumblebee Blues* a pick-up measure or the first full measure of the song?

Right Hand

- Circle the five-finger positions given in the right hand. The first one, at the beginning of the piece, is done for you.
- Clap and count the following swing rhythms: (refer to page 15 if needed)

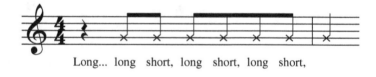

Long... long short, long short, long short,

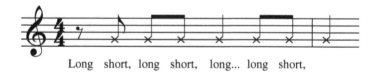

Long short, long short, long... long short,

- The second rhythm above can be found in measures _____ and _____. Play them.
- Play measure 10, excerpted below, several times, making sure to use the correct fingering:

buz - zin' like a bum - ble bee. ___

Left Hand

- Play the three triads in this piece.

- Circle the quarter rests 𝄽 that occur on beat one in the left hand. There are five altogether.

Bumblebee Blues

Words and Music by
Luann Carman

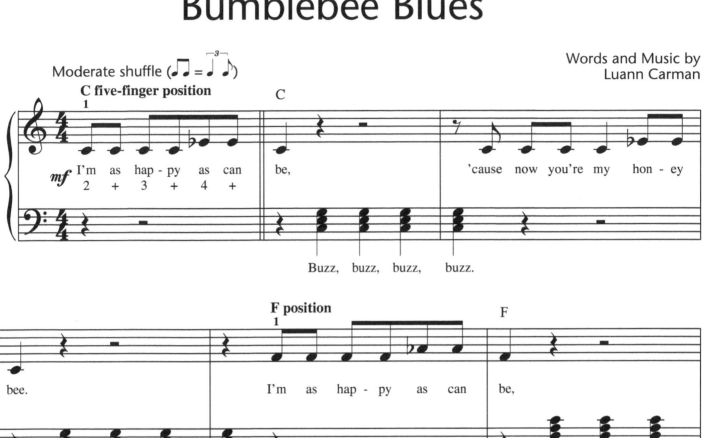

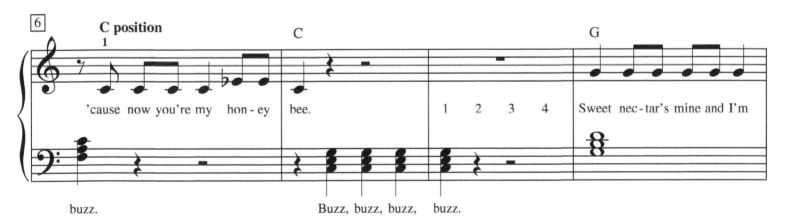

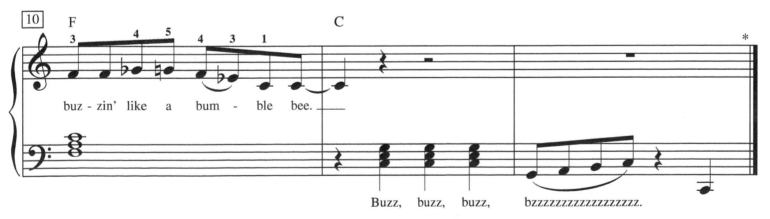

*Measure 12 would ordinarily be a partial measure, allowing the missing beats to be borrowed for the pick-up measure.
However, in jazz and blues music, composers and arrangers don't follow this rule unless there is a repeat.

Shake, Rattle And Roll Worksheet

Write in the chord symbols for *Shake, Rattle And Roll*. It's a C blues. However, the chords in measures 9 and 10 are D minor7 – G7 (IIm7 – V7), not G7 – F7 (V7 – IV7), as we have studied so far. Using **chord substitutions**, which simply means replacing one chord with another, is a technique which is often used in the blues. (See *Glossary of Terms*, page 58.)

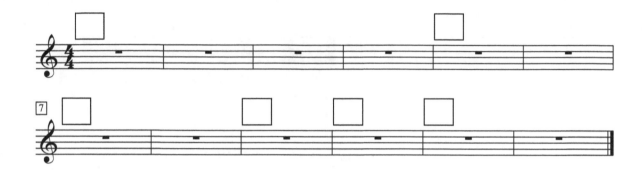

Left Hand Warm-Up

If you've played *Walkin'-Bass Blues* at the beginning of the book, this walking bass should be familiar to you.

- Walk the bass!

- Now play the same pattern in F:

Right Hand Warm-Up

Remember the discussion of riffs on page 14? The melody of *Shake, Rattle And Roll* is based on the 1-bar riff below. It repeats 4 times, sometimes with a slight variation.

- Play the excerpts below. Don't forget to count!

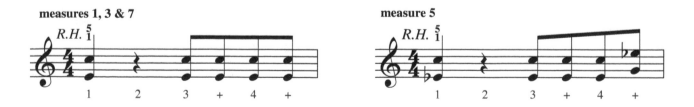

Shake, Rattle And Roll

Words and Music by
Charles Calhoun

Hound Dog Worksheet

- Fill in the chord symbols for D blues. (Refer to page 7 if needed.)

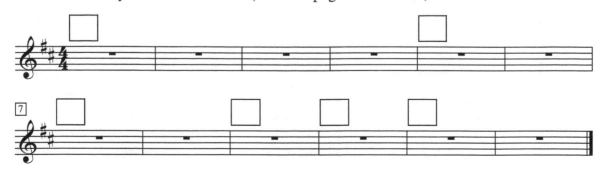

- Is the beginning of *Hound Dog* the pick-up measure or the first full measure of the song?

Right Hand

The right-hand melody, measure 1 through measure 4 below, repeats later in the piece.

- Which measures repeat this phrase? Measure _____ through _____.

You ain't noth-in' but a hound dog cry - in' all the time.
  + 2 + 3 + 4 + 1 + 2 + 3 + 4 + 1 + 2 + 3 + 4 + 1

a. Circle the fingerings on the Fs in the excerpt above.
b. Clap and count the excerpt.
c. Play the excerpt.

Left Hand – Grace Notes

Normally, grace notes are played just before the main note. However, it is far too easy to get thrown off rhythmically if you don't have much experience with them. At first, you might like to try "crushing" the grace note and the main note at the same time, then releasing the grace note quickly while continuing to hold the main note of the melody.

Play the left-hand D chord below. The fingering (1–2–5) is different from what you might expect for a root-position chord. This unconventional fingering will prepare you to add grace notes later.

> **Grace notes** are notes that are added to the main notes of a phrase. They can be found in melodies and in accompaniments. Grace notes are written in a smaller note size, preceding the main note.
>
>

Play the D chord in the following rhythm:

Now add the grace notes.

Practice *Hound Dog*, hands together, without the left-hand grace notes. When you can do this with the correct rhythm and without hesitation, add the grace notes.

Hound Dog

Words and Music by
Jerry Leiber and Mike Stoller

* Practice hands together without the left-hand grace notes. When you can do this with the correct rhythm and without
hesitation, add the grace notes.

Blue Suede Shoes Worksheet

Fill in the chord symbols for F blues. (Refer to page 6 if needed).

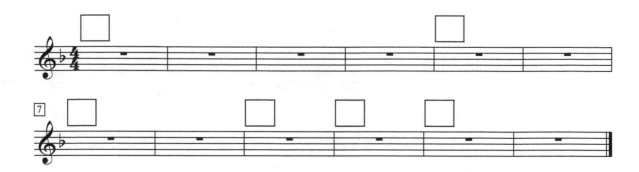

Left-Hand Warm-Up

- Play the 7ths below.

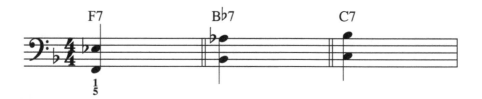

- Play the walking-bass pattern on F.

- Now transpose it to B-flat.

In the score…
- Circle all the fingering indicated for the right hand.
- Circle the rests in measures 5, 9, and 10.
- Practice the advanced rhythm for measure 6.

Blue Suede Shoes

Words and Music by
Carl Lee Perkins

Jailhouse Rock Worksheet

This is a 16-bar blues. There are four extra measures of I at the beginning of the song. The traditional 12-bar blues pattern begins at measure 5.

Write in the chord symbols for this 16-bar D blues.

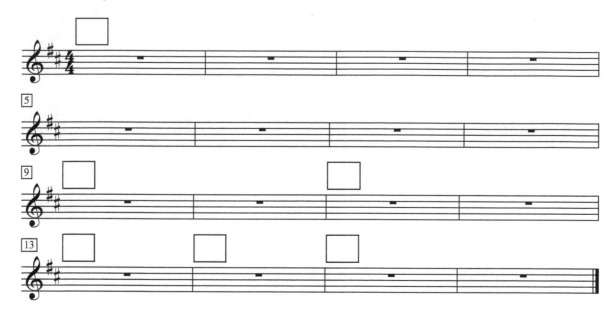

Left Hand

- Practice the three blues chords in this key. Instead of triads, these are 7ths.

- Indicate which measures have 7ths in the left hand: __1__, ____, ____, ____, ____, and ____.

- With your teacher, play and count the example at right several times.

- Indicate the measures in which this riff occurs: __2__ – __3__, ____ – ____, and ____ – ____.

- Play this walking-bass pattern in D.

- Now transpose it to G.

Right Hand

This melody has only four notes. Here is your right-hand position. Find your hand position and be sure not to change your fingering as you play the entire song.

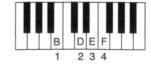

Jailhouse Rock

Words and Music by
Jerry Leiber and Mike Stoller

Tutti Frutti Worksheet

In this tune, there is a two-measure introduction, so there are 14 measures, not 12. The 12-bar blues pattern begins at measure 3.

- Write in the chord symbols for G 12-bar blues. (Refer to page 7 if needed.)

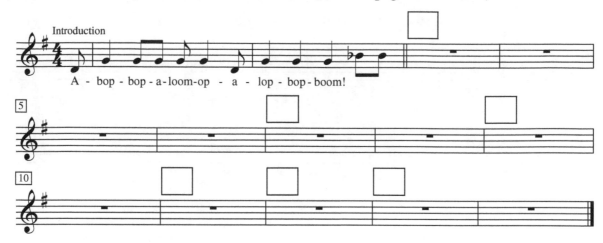

- Play the introduction, above: *"A-bop-bop-a-loom-op-a-lop-bop-boom!"*
- Where does this fun riff, *"A-bop-bop-a-loom-op-a-lop-bop-boom!"* repeat?
  Measures _____ and _____.

Right Hand

Keep your right hand in a G minor finger position from measure 3 through measure 12.

Remember the discussion of *riff melody* on page 14? The melody of *Tutti Frutti* is based on the 2-bar riff below.

- Clap this rhythm.

- In what other measures does this rhythm appear?

  Measures _____ & _____, _____ & _____, _____ & _____, and _____ & _____.

Left Hand

- Play this walking-bass pattern.

- Play the same pattern on C.

- Now, play it on D, but this time play *only* the first four notes.

Tutti Frutti

Words and Music by
Little Richard Penniman and Dorothy La Bostrie

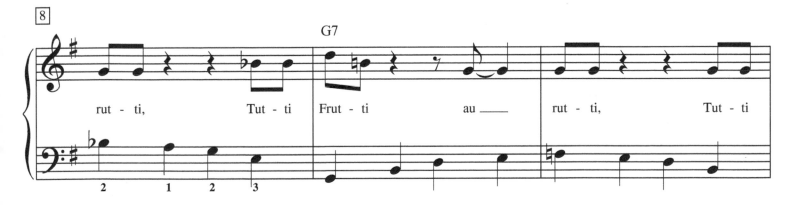

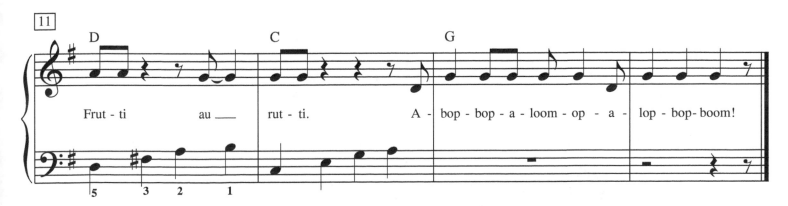

In The Mood Worksheet

- Write in the standard chord symbols for a G blues.

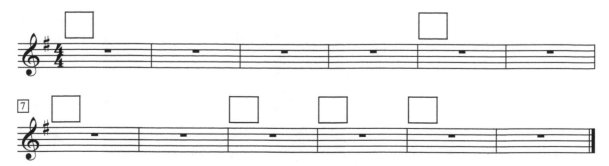

- Write in the chord symbols below for *In The Mood*.

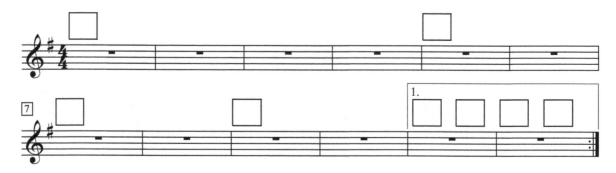

- Which measures are different from the standard 12-bar blues? Measures ____, ____, and ____.

Left Hand

The G–C–A–D (I–IV–II–V) progression in measures 11–12 is a good example of a **turnaround**.

Note the left-hand rhythm and intervals in measures 1–2.

> A **turnaround** is a chord progression that fills in at the end of a 12-bar blues form, allowing the player to "turn around" and go back to the beginning of the form. The progression, usually two bars long, leads back to the I chord.

a. The same rhythm and interval pattern can be found in measures _____ – ____, _____ – ____, and _____ – ____.

b. Are there ties or slurs in these measures? _____

c. Play each of these two-measure patterns once.

Right Hand

- Play these chords:
- Identify them as I, IV, or V chords in the blanks below the chords.
- Now play each chord "broken" several times without hesitating between repetitions.

Find these broken-chord patterns in the music. Circle the first broken chord of each group. Now play the right-hand part with accents. Don't overdo it. Make them subtle.

In The Mood

By Joe Garland

Jump, Jive An' Wail Worksheet

Left Hand

Practice the following walking-bass patterns.

m. 1-2

m. 5-6

m. 9-12

m. 13-14

Right Hand

Play the following two-note chords.
Note the fingering.

Rhythm

Clap these rhythms.

m. 1

1. This rhythm appears in measures __1__, ____, ____, ____, and ____.

m. 2

2. This rhythm appears in measures __2__, ____, ____, and ____.

m. 10

3. How are measures 2 and 10 different?

Practice Tips

Clap on your lap, with your left hand clapping the bass-clef part and your right hand clapping the treble-clef part. Now play both hands on the keyboard, listening carefully to your left hand. Be sure to play steady quarter notes, particularly on beat one of each measure.

Jump, Jive An' Wail

Words and Music by
Louis Prima

33

I Got You (I Feel Good) Worksheet

This tune has 18 bars, with two extra measures at the beginning and four at the end, to accommodate a very famous riff. The 12-bar progression begins on measure 3.

Write in the chord symbols for D 12-bar blues.

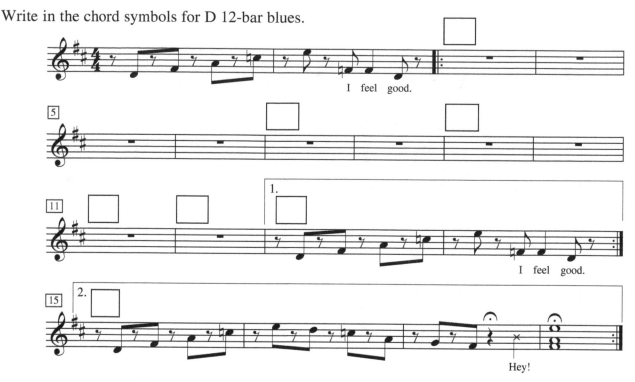

All notes that don't have lyrics are imitating horn parts. Imagine hearing the sound of horns as you play those parts. You probably will want to make them slightly softer than the melody line because they are an accompaniment. Let's practice these horn lines, excerpted below, to hear them well and to tackle some of the fingering!

* A 9th chord simply adds the 9th note of the scale to the chord. For the D9 chords in this tune, the 9th is an E.

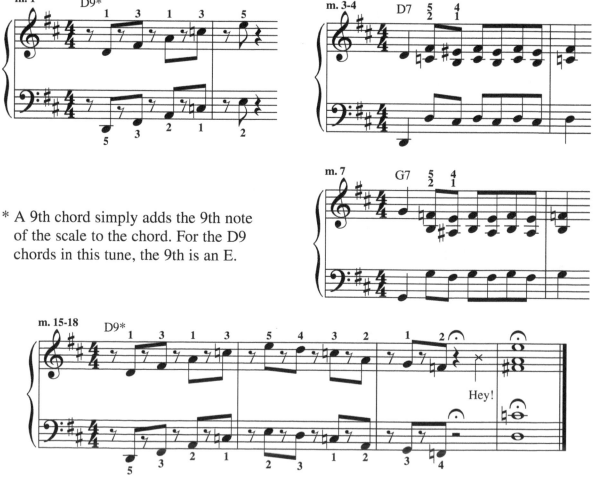

34

I Got You (I Feel Good)

Words and Music by
James Brown

Night Train Worksheet

This tune is 24 measures, repeating the 12-bar blues progression twice. The melody, however, completely changes at measure 13, the start of the second 12-bar progression.

Write in the chord symbols for G blues.

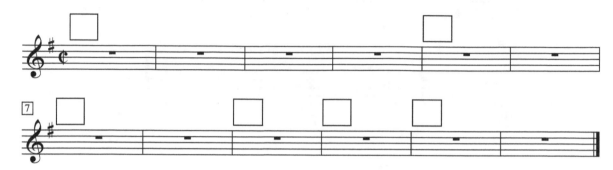

Right-Hand Melody

We already mentioned that this tune has two different melodies. Both melodies have three phrases, typical of a 12-bar blues melody, as we studied on page 14. However, in this tune the third phrase does not change, which is not typical.

Write out the two different melodies below and then play them.

First melody, measures 1–4:

What is different about the third phrase of this melody (measures 9–12)?

Second melody, pick-up and measures 13–16:

Read through the lyrics. Do these lyric phrases follow the expected pattern for blues lyrics?

YES   NO   Why? _____

_____

How does this tune sound like a train? Circle your answer below.
   a. The first two notes of the melody, on the words *Night Train,* could be an imitation of a train whistle.
   b. The left hand repeated eighth-note pattern during the first 12 bars.
   c. The repeated eighth-note pattern of the second melody, measure 13.
   d. All of the above.

Night Train

Words by Oscar Washington and Lewis C. Simpkins
Music by Jimmy Forrest

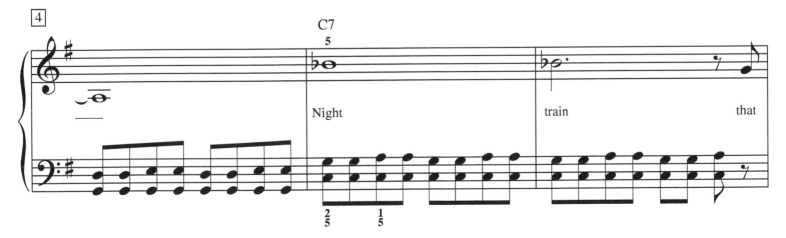

PART III:

An Introduction to Improvising the Blues

The exercises in this section are progressive and are designed to give you a taste of what improvising is all about. They begin with short, easy-to-master improvisations—first on the black keys, and then on D blues scales. These exercises have teacher accompaniments that fill in with a steady rhythmic pattern and chord progression. You have to supply only the improvised melody in these early exercises. Later exercises ask you to improvise a melody *and* play a left-hand accompaniment.

When you improvise a melody, the notes are not supplied for you. Come up with them yourself, and that will be a new experience. Don't be shy! Even your very first improvisations will sound terrific if you follow the instructions for each exercise. After a few practice runs, you will begin to feel very comfortable and will have more confidence in your ability to be creative. This is the heart of improvisation. You are not only interpreting the music, you are creating it as well. Keep an open mind, and let your imagination take the lead as you play.

Remember: there are no wrong notes when you improvise, only more opportunities to create new melodies!

Exercise 1: Black-Key Improvisation

Black-Key Blues, on the following page, is an improvisation exercise for the right hand alone, played on the black keys.

Your teacher will play an accompaniment (written out on the next page) as you improvise a melody. This accompaniment is like the rhythm section (bass, drums, and keyboard, or guitar) of a band. Your teacher will play a bass line and chords (like a pianist or guitarist would play), and will provide a strong, steady rhythmic pulse (like a drummer would play).

Right-Hand Improvisation

You will play only black keys in the right hand. Your left hand plays nothing in this exercise. This is a black-key improvisation, so you don't have to think about a particular set of notes or a scale. It's a lot of fun just to "jam" away!

- Play rhythmically. The accompaniment part is quite "bluesy" and rhythmic, so listen carefully to the accompaniment, matching the style you hear.

- Repeat this improvisation exercise several times, until you get the feel for improvising, and can enjoy creating different melodies above the accompaniment. Once you feel comfortable improvising in this way, you are ready to take the next step.

- Once the above feels easy, try adding an A-natural as a passing tone between A-flat and B-flat. You are now improvising over an **E-flat blues scale**.

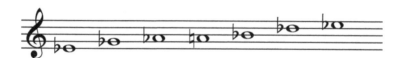

Black-Key Blues

Student: Improvise on the black keys, using your right hand in the upper register of the piano.

Exercise 2: White-Key Improvisation, the D Dorian Scale

In the key of D, you can play a blues improvisation using only white keys by improvising on the D Dorian scale. Playing a blues on this scale will give you a more jazzy sound, because it contains the 9th (E) and the 13th (B).

Learn the following scales with straight eighths first, then practice "swinging" them.

Right Hand

- Play the following scale, a D Dorian. It is played using only white keys and starts and ends on D.

- Now play the D Dorian scale in two octaves.

- Learn the D Dorian scale, three octaves.*

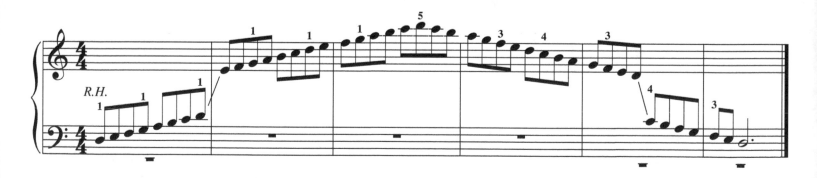

* You may choose to do this later, after you've gained some experience improvising within a two-octave range. You'll find that adding a third octave will allow for more flexible and varied improvisational ideas.

Exercise 3: Improvising a Right-Hand Melody in D Dorian

Right Hand

- Improvise a melody on the D Dorian scale, using one, two, or three octaves. Your teacher will play the Teacher Accompaniment for *Improvisation Train*.

Improvisation Train

If you would like to spend more time improvising on the Dorian scale, you may choose to skip to Exercise 8, returning to exercises 5–7 at a later time.

Exercise 4: The D Minor Pentatonic Scale

Right Hand

- Now play the same D Dorian scale, but omit the E and B, This is called the D minor pentatonic scale. Pay close attention to the suggested fingering.

- Play the same D minor pentatonic scale two octaves, all in the right hand.

- Learn the D minor pentatonic scale, three octaves.*

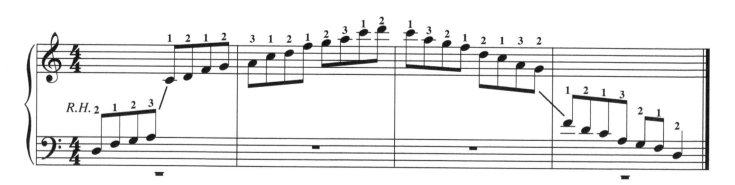

* As we discussed with the three-octave Dorian scale, you may choose to add a third octave at a later time. Get comfortable improvising within a two-octave range, then add the third octave. Remember, adding a third octave will allow for more improvisational ideas.

Exercise 5: Improvising a D Blues on the D Minor Pentatonic Scale

Right Hand

- Improvise a melody on the **D minor pentatonic scale** while your teacher plays the Teacher Accompaniment to *Improvisation Train* (page 43).

Exercise 6: The D Blues Scale

Of all three scales (the Dorian, minor pentatonic, and blues scale), the blues scale will give you the most "bluesy" sound. The reason for this is that not only are the 3rd and 7th flatted, but the 5th is, as well.

Right Hand

- Play the D minor pentatonic scale again, but add an A-flat. This is a **D blues scale**.

- Now play the D blues scale, two octaves.

- Learn the D blues scale, three octaves. As with the three-octave Dorian and D minor pentatonic scales, the three-octave D blues scale can be learned at a later time. Improvise within two octaves first, until it feels easy, and then move on to three octaves.

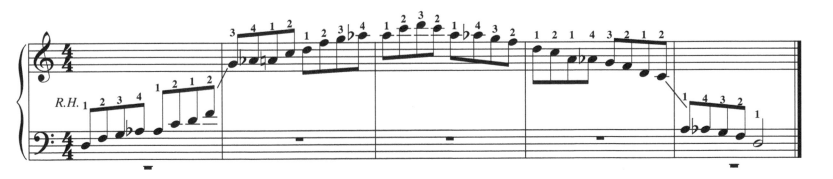

Exercise 7: D Blues for the Right Hand Alone

Right Hand

- Improvise a melody using the D blues scale while your teacher plays the Teacher Accompaniment for *Improvisation Train* (page 43).

Exercise 8: D Blues for the Left Hand Alone

Left Hand

- Play the D blues progression below. Practice this progression until it feels "good," then MEMORIZE IT!

D Blues

(write your title here)*

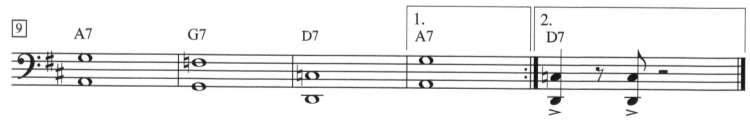

*Although you are always improvising something new, title your work. Perhaps call it something simple, like _Annie's Improv_, or something more descriptive, such as _Nick's Memphis City Blues_ or _Collin's Bad Cat Blues_.

46

Exercise 9: Hands Together

Once you have memorized the left-hand D blues progression (Exercise 8) and you've practiced your D Dorian, D minor pentatonic, and/or D Blues scale(s) until you can play them with ease and accuracy, it's time to begin to improvise hands together.

Practice Tip

- Practice slowly, focusing on the left-hand continuity (no hesitating). Keep the right-hand improvisation simple, using only one or two notes per measure, to begin with. Use the sample notes given in the exercise to help you get started.

Right Hand

- Improvise on the D Dorian, D minor pentatonic, or D blues scale, whichever one you prefer.
- Begin by using only one-octave scales, then expand to two, and eventually three, octaves.
- The following page has starting notes from the minor pentatonic and blues scales. However, any of the three scales will work for your improvisation.
- As you get more comfortable with your right-hand improvisation, you may notice that you change the starting notes or omit them altogether. If this happens, see where it takes your improvisation. If you like the sound, you can always use them again on the next try.

Left Hand

- Play the D Blues progression (Exercise 8). The following page has sample notes to help get you started with this exercise.

On page 49, there is a *D Blues Improvisation Model*. It has the same sample notes you will use, but the remaining measures are filled in with improvisational ideas. This will give you an opportunity to hear what another player has improvised with the same sample notes. Ask your teacher to play this solo for you, or, if you'd like, work on it and learn it yourself.

D Blues Improvisation

Create you own improvisation in the blank measures. Notice that some measures have sample, improvised notes to help you out.

Tip: Stay above treble C in this measure because you'll be playing a high A in the very next measure.

Tip: Connect measures 10 & 12 by playing some descending scale notes, from high G down to the D above middle C.

D Blues Improvisation Model

Expanding on Your D Blues Improvisation

I hope you are having a lot of fun improvising with the exercises so far. In the next exercises, you'll find a few more left-hand accompaniments. Each new accompaniment is designed to assist you with new right-hand skills. You'll also find more ideas for your right-hand improvisations. Since the exercises are progressive, it's best to play them in the order given.

Exercise 10: Keep the Beat

The next left-hand accompaniment is designed to help you keep time, with exactly four beats in each measure, and to make sure you are feeling those beats evenly.

Practice Tip

- First, play the left hand alone.
- Then, play the exercise through once again, adding your right-hand improvisation as you did in the previous exercises. There are some right-hand starting notes in this exercise to help you get going.
- Remember, if you spontaneously alter the starting notes while you are improvising, let it happen.

Exercise 11: Improvisation

R.H.: Improvise on the D dorian, Dm pentatonic, or D blues scales.

Exercise 12: Let's Improvise More Melodies

A good improviser will start with a single melodic idea and then will expand on it. Let's briefly review the basic characteristics of blues melodies and lyrics.

There are three melodic phrases, four measures each, in the 12-bar blues:

First phrase (measures 1–4): is played over the I chord.

Second phrase (measures 5–8): often repeats the first phrase. Even though the melody here may be identical to the first phrase, the harmony changes to the IV chord, giving the phrase a different sound.

Third phrase (measures 9–12): completes the musical sentence, and sounds like an ending to the first two phrases. The harmonic progression leads from the V chord, to the IV and finally, ends on I.

For example, take a look at *School Day Blues*.

School Day Blues

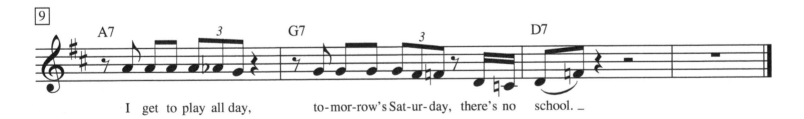

The blues lyrics formula will help you to improvise. Let's quickly review:

First phrase: an introductory lyric line

Second phrase: repeats the first line

Third phrase: the rhythmic word pattern changes, and the new lyrics complete the thought

Again, the second phrase is the same as the first. Make up your own lyrics and—surprise!—a melody will appear! You can make the words silly, or "down-and-out," as in *School Day Blues*. In *Exercise 13: Improvisation*, create your lyric lines first, writing them into the music staff over the given bass line. Then, improvise a melody that fits your lyrics.

Exercise 13: Improvisation

_____
(write your title here)

R.H.: Improvise a melody using the D dorian, Dm pentatonic, or D blues scales.

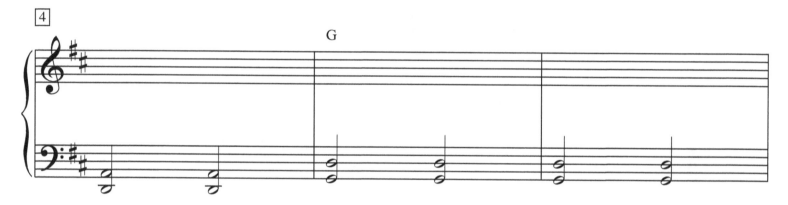

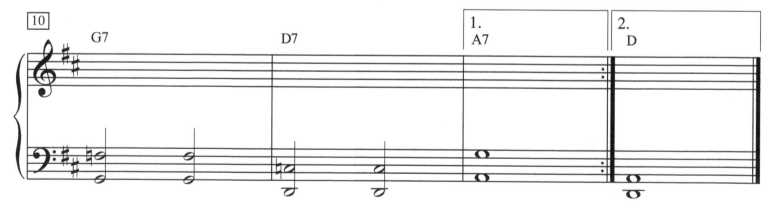

Use this space to work out your lyric lines before placing them into the music.

Phrase 1:_____

Phrase 2:_____

Phrase 3:_____

Sample Improvisation, Analyzed

Transcriptions are usually taken down, or transcribed, from audio recordings by famous performers. There are many books that are available in which the improvisations of famous jazz and blues performers are written out in standard music notation for others to analyze and learn.

Analyzing transcriptions is an effective tool in learning to improvise a good solo. The following analysis is for the sample improvisation you played earlier. We will look at these features: scale choices, blues melody, blues riffs, and building a solo.

Scales

This improvisation uses notes from the D minor pentatonic and D blues scales. I chose these scales because they have a more "bluesy" sound. I didn't choose the D Dorian scale because it has the 9th and 13th, which would have given it a more "jazzy" sound. Notice that measure 7 contains the Dm pentatonic scale in its most basic form.

Melody

The shaded notes in the first two measures of each line bear a striking resemblance to *School Day Blues* melody, Exercise 12. This is an example of how to incorporate a known melody into your solo.

Building A Solo

A good solo starts out simply and gradually adds more excitement. About two-thirds of the way through, this solo "peaks" (measures 8–9), and then winds down again toward the end.

Riffs

Measures 1, 2, 4, 5, 6, 8, 11, and 12 contain blues riffs (highlighted). A **riff** is a musical idea, or a motif, that has a particular stylistic sound to it; for example, blues, country, or jazz style.

Sample Improvisation, Analyzed

Exercise 14: Practice Those Riffs

Practice the blues riffs in *Improvisation 14* by themselves. Use them in your own improvisations.

It's true that when improvising, fingering is improvised as well. However, it's important to develop good FINGERING HABITS, so choose reliable fingerings for riffs and always practice them with that same fingering. This will help them to become automatic as you improvise in any key. Jazz and blues musicians spend hours practicing special riffs in all keys so they can use them in performances, spontaneously. It's not true that jazz and blues musicians don't practice. They do—a lot!

Exercise 15: You're Ready for the Blues

You are ready for a challenge: a completely improvised blues solo!

Remember that in most blues piano-playing the left hand plays a simple idea or a repetitive pattern. You shouldn't have to think about that hand very much. This allows you to focus on the more challenging right-hand improvisation.

Performance Tips

Right Hand

Improvise on the scale of your choice: the D Dorian, Dm pentatonic, or D blues.

Start with a simple melody, like you did in the previous exercise, and then elaborate on it. Expand your ideas, using two, and eventually three, octaves.

Be expressive and play within the style.

Left Hand

Use the left-hand part for *Improvisation Train* (page 43).

Keep a steady, rhythmic beat.

Practice your left-hand part first, then add your improvised melody.

Exercise 16: Expanding Your Improvisations

Hound Dog and *Jailhouse Rock* are in the key of D. Play through the first ending of either tune, then take a solo (improvise) for 12 bars using the left-hand accompaniment from Exercise 9 (page 47) or Exercise 11 (page 50), then return to the tune and finish with the second ending.

Some Final Words About Blues Improvisation

Listen

Listening is a very important part of studying music. Musicians like guitarist BB King and pianists Oscar Peterson and Gene Harris are great blues improvisers. Listen to some of their recordings. Attend blues concerts (making sure there is a keyboard player in the group!). If there isn't someone on piano, listen to the lead guitarist or soloist on horns to get ideas for your right hand. Listen to the bassist for left-hand ideas. The advice I hear most often from many fine improvisers is "Listen."

Learn from the great performers

Studying transcriptions of great improvisations is another important tool in learning to improvise. Transcriptions can sometimes be found in music stores, but often they have to be ordered. Go in with a list of your favorite blues artists and ask what's available.

Play transcriptions and learn from them. Find the melodic phrases. Perhaps you might take some of the catchy phrases and use them in your own improvisation, as we did in Exercise 15. Notice how the solo sections start out simply and gradually build to a climax, or peak. Notice how other styles do this, too.

Study the formulas

Form, form, and formulas! We have learned that there is a formula for the melody, harmony, and lyrics. There is also a common formula for the entire performance of a tune. For example, a 12-bar blues has a lot more than just 12 bars in it! There will be an introduction, a statement of the tune (with the original melody), solos (perhaps a guitar solo, horn solo, or piano solo), and an ending. When the soloist plays, he plays over the harmony of the original 12-bar tune, without the melody, of course–he is improvising his own melody! The guitarist, for example, often solos over several choruses. In other words, one chorus is 12 bars, so a soloist may improvise over the 12-bar harmony several times, making it a 12-, 24-, or a 36-bar solo, perhaps even more.

Below is a sample outline of a complete performance of a blues tune:

Introduction

Statement of the melody

Solos: Guitar (usually 2-3 choruses)
       Horn, saxophone for example, also 2-3 choruses
       Piano, several chorus as well

Return to the original melody

Ending: This is optional. (Often the tune will end on the last note of a 12-bar chorus)

This outline should help you to hear what's going on as you listen to a complete performance of a blues tune. The songs in this book offer the original "statement of the melody" and perhaps an introduction and ending. Usually a musician will play the tune as written (more or less!), take a solo, return to the original melody, and then play an ending.

Other blues styles use different song forms. For example, a 1950s blues tune may have a verse, where the lyrics tell most of the story, and a *chorus*, the 12-bar blues section (usually the most familiar part of the song). In an effort to have only one, fairly-easy type of chord progression for this entire book (the 12-bar blues), I have left out the verses. In this song form, solos would most likely be taken over the 12-bar blues section of the tune.

Have fun!

I hope you have enjoyed playing the blues in this book. It's important to remember that the improvisation section of this book is just an introduction. If you wish to continue studying, consult more books on the subject, ones that will teach you to play in new keys and that will offer new accompaniment ideas and blues riffs for the right hand. Listen to great improvisers, and study transcriptions. Whether you are playing from a sheet of music or improvising, have fun! It will make a positive difference in your music-making.

Glossary of Terms

The **blues scale** is created by starting with a major scale and selecting these notes: root, flat-3, 4, flat-5, 5, flat-7, 8.

A **chord substitution** simply replaces one chord with another. Chords have a function within a progression; for example, the V7 chord usually resolves to the I chord, the II and IV chords sound pleasing when progressing to the V chord, etc. Some chords, because they have several notes in common, are so closely related that one can be substituted for another without changing the essential function. The effect is a subtle change in sound.

In other cases, a chord substitution may be completely unrelated to the original chord, thus altering the function. For example, if a V chord is substituted for I chord, the V chord will not sound resolved, whereas the I chord did. In the blues, measure 12 is often a V chord instead of a I chord when "turning around" and playing another chorus (see, for example, the first ending of *Jump, Jive An' Wail*, page 33).

A **gig** is a musician's term for a performance engagement by a soloist or a band.

Grace notes are notes that are added to the main notes of a phrase. They can be found in melodies and in accompaniments. Grace notes are written in a smaller note size, preceding the main note.

A **passing tone** is a note that comes between two other notes and moves in the same direction.

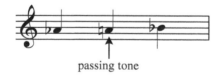

passing tone

A **pick-up** is an incomplete measure that occurs before the first full measure.

A **progression** is a set sequence of chords that follows a predictable and logical pattern. The **12-bar blues progression** uses the I^7, IV^7, and V^7 chords of any key in a distinctive chord sequence over 12 measures.

Measure 1–4	Measures 5–6	Measures 7–8	Measure 9	Measure 10	Measures 11–12
I^7	IV^7	I^7	V^7	IV^7	I^7

A **riff** is a short melodic idea which has a particular stylistic sound to it; for example, blues, country, or jazz style.

Straight eighths are pairs of eighth notes which are played "as written," with equal value. They are often used in rock blues tunes such as *Jailhouse Rock* (page 27) and *I Got You (I Feel Good)* (page 35).

Swing eighths refers to eighth-note pairs which are written as even eighths (♪♪), but are played as a triplet figure (♪♪). Playing swing eighths is sometimes referred to as playing a **shuffle rhythm**.

A **transcription** is a note-for-note copy, written in standard music notation, of an improvisation.

To **transpose** is to play a song in a different key than the one in which it was written. This is usually done without writing out the song in the new key. Instead, most jazz and blues musicians transpose using a combination of "by ear" playing and knowing the common patterns of the musical style.

A **blues turnaround** is a chord progression that fills in at the end of a 12-bar blues form, allowing the player to "turn around" and go back to the beginning of the form. The progression, usually two bars long, leads back to the I chord. (A common turnaround: I–VI–ii–V.)

A **walking-bass pattern** is a bass line of steady quarter-notes or eighth-notes, usually moving stepwise and following the I–IV–V chord progression.

Answers

Part I: What is the Blues?

Page 7, Exercise 1
Chord symbols for G blues: G, C, G, D, C, G
Chord symbols for D blues: D, G, D, A, G, D

Page 13, Exercise 7
First phrase: You ain't nothin' but a hound dog,
cryin' all the time.
Second phrase: You ain't nothin' but a hound dog,
cryin' all the time.
Third phrase: Well, you ain't never caught a rabbit
and you ain't no friend of mine.

Page 14, Exercise 8
First phrase

Second phrase

Third phrase

Page 14, The Riff:

Part II: Classic Blues Tunes and Worksheets

Page 18, *Bumblebee Blues* Worksheet
Chord symbols for C blues: C, F, C, G, F, C
The beginning is a pick-up measure.
RH: The second rhythm indicated for the RH
can be found in measures 2 and 6.
LH: The quarter rests on beat 1 should be circled
in measures 1, 3, 5, 7, and 11.

Page 20, *Shake, Rattle and Roll* Worksheet
Chord symbols for *Shake, Rattle and Roll:*
C7, F7, C7, Dm7, G7, C7

Page 22, *Hound Dog* Worksheet
Chord symbols for D blues: D, G, D, A7, G7, D
The beginning is actually a pick-up measure, because there
are not four complete beats.
RH: Measure 5 through measure 8.

Page 24, *Blue Suede Shoes* Worksheet
Chord symbols for F blues: F7, B♭7, F7, C7, B♭7, F

Page 26, *Jailhouse Rock* Worksheet
Chord symbols for D blues: D7, G7, D7, A7, G7, D7
LH: The measures which have 7ths are 1, 13, 14, 15, 16,
and 17 (2nd ending).
The riff occurs in measures 2–3, 4–5, and 6–7.

Page 28, *Tutti Frutti* Worksheet
Chord symbols for G blues: G7, C7, G7, D, C, G
A-bop-bop-a-loom-op-a-lo-bop-boom repeats in measures
13 and 14. Because these measures extend beyond the
12-bar blues form, it is considered a tag ending.
RH: The indicated rhythm appears in measures 5–6, 7–8,
9–10, and 11–12.

Page 30, *In The Mood* Worksheet
Chord symbols for G blues: G, C, G, D, C, G
Chord symbols for *In The Mood:* G, C, G, D, G, C, A, D7
Measures 10, 11, and 12 are different from a standard
12-bar blues.
LH: Measures 3–4, 5–6, 7–8, and 9–10. There are ties in
these measures.
RH: G, C, D.
In the music, circle the first three notes in measures 1, 5, 7,
and 9.

Page 32, *Jump, Jive An' Wail* Worksheet
Rhythm
1. This rhythm appears in measures 1, 3, 5, 7, and 9.
2. This rhythm appears in measures 2, 4, 6, and 8.
3. Measures 2 and 10 are different in that measure 10 has
a quarter note on beat 3 rather than two eighth notes.

Page 34, *I Got You* Worksheet
Chord symbols for D blues: D7, G7, D7, A7, G7, D7

Page 36, *Night Train* Worksheet
Chord symbols for G blues: G, C, G, D, C7, G
First melody

Second melody

Lyrics
YES. The lyrics follow the expected pattern for blues lyrics
because the first two lines are the same and the third line
is different, suggesting to resolve the dilemma of the first
two lines.

How does this tune sound like a train?
d. All of the above.

COMPOSER SHOWCASE
HAL·LEONARD STUDENT PIANO LIBRARY

This series showcases great original piano music from our **Hal Leonard Student Piano Library** family of composers. Carefully graded for easy selection.

BILL BOYD

JAZZ BITS (AND PIECES)
Early Intermediate Level
00290312 11 Solos.............................$7.99

JAZZ DELIGHTS
Intermediate Level
00240435 11 Solos.............................$8.99

JAZZ FEST
Intermediate Level
00240436 10 Solos.............................$8.99

JAZZ PRELIMS
Early Elementary Level
00290032 12 Solos.............................$7.99

JAZZ SKETCHES
Intermediate Level
00220001 8 Solos...............................$8.99

JAZZ STARTERS
Elementary Level
00290425 10 Solos.............................$7.99

JAZZ STARTERS II
Late Elementary Level
00290434 11 Solos.............................$7.99

JAZZ STARTERS III
Late Elementary Level
00290465 12 Solos.............................$8.99

THINK JAZZ!
Early Intermediate Level
00290417 Method Book.....................$12.99

TONY CARAMIA

JAZZ MOODS
Intermediate Level
00296728 8 Solos...............................$6.95

SUITE DREAMS
Intermediate Level
00296775 4 Solos...............................$6.99

SONDRA CLARK

THREE ODD METERS
Intermediate Level
00296472 3 Duets...............................$6.95

MATTHEW EDWARDS

CONCERTO FOR YOUNG PIANISTS
FOR 2 PIANOS, FOUR HANDS
Intermediate Level Book/CD
00296356 3 Movements $19.99

CONCERTO NO. 2 IN G MAJOR
FOR 2 PIANOS, 4 HANDS
Intermediate Level Book/CD
00296670 3 Movements......................$17.99

PHILLIP KEVEREN

MOUSE ON A MIRROR
Late Elementary Level
00296361 5 Solos...............................$8.99

MUSICAL MOODS
Elementary/Late Elementary Level
00296714 7 Solos...............................$6.99

SHIFTY-EYED BLUES
Late Elementary Level
00296374 5 Solos...............................$7.99

CAROL KLOSE

THE BEST OF CAROL KLOSE
Early Intermediate to Late Intermediate Level
00146151 15 Solos.............................$12.99

CORAL REEF SUITE
Late Elementary Level
00296354 7 Solos...............................$7.50

DESERT SUITE
Intermediate Level
00296667 6 Solos...............................$7.99

FANCIFUL WALTZES
Early Intermediate Level
00296473 5 Solos...............................$7.95

GARDEN TREASURES
Late Intermediate Level
00296787 5 Solos...............................$8.50

ROMANTIC EXPRESSIONS
Intermediate/Late Intermediate Level
00296923 5 Solos...............................$8.99

WATERCOLOR MINIATURES
Early Intermediate Level
00296848 7 Solos...............................$7.99

JENNIFER LINN

AMERICAN IMPRESSIONS
Intermediate Level
00296471 6 Solos...............................$8.99

ANIMALS HAVE FEELINGS TOO
Early Elementary/Elementary Level
00147789 8 Solos...............................$8.99

CHRISTMAS IMPRESSIONS
Intermediate Level
00296706 8 Solos...............................$8.99

JUST PINK
Elementary Level
00296722 9 Solos...............................$8.99

LES PETITES IMAGES
Late Elementary Level
00296664 7 Solos...............................$8.99

LES PETITES IMPRESSIONS
Intermediate Level
00296355 6 Solos...............................$7.99

REFLECTIONS
Late Intermediate Level
00296843 5 Solos...............................$8.99

TALES OF MYSTERY
Intermediate Level
00296769 6 Solos...............................$8.99

LYNDA LYBECK-ROBINSON

ALASKA SKETCHES
Early Intermediate Level
00119637 8 Solos...............................$7.99

AN AWESOME ADVENTURE
Late Elementary Level
00137563...$7.99

FOR THE BIRDS
Early Intermediate/Intermediate Level
00237078 ....$8.99

WHISPERING WOODS
Late Elementary Level
00275905 9 Solos...............................$8.99

MONA REJINO

CIRCUS SUITE
Late Elementary Level
00296665 5 Solos...............................$6.99

COLOR WHEEL
Early Intermediate Level
00201951 6 Solos...............................$8.99

JUST FOR KIDS
Elementary Level
00296840 8 Solos...............................$7.99

MERRY CHRISTMAS MEDLEYS
Intermediate Level
00296799 5 Solos...............................$8.99

MINIATURES IN STYLE
Intermediate Level
00148088 6 Solos...............................$8.99

PORTRAITS IN STYLE
Early Intermediate Level
00296507 6 Solos...............................$8.99

EUGÉNIE ROCHEROLLE

CELEBRATION SUITE
Intermediate Level
00152724 3 Duets (1 Piano, 4 Hands)...............$8.99

**ENCANTOS ESPAÑOLES
(SPANISH DELIGHTS)**
Intermediate Level
00125451 6 Solos...............................$8.99

JAMBALAYA
Intermediate Level
00296654 Ensemble (2 Pianos, 8 Hands).........$12.99

JAMBALAYA
Intermediate Level
00296725 Piano Duo (2 Pianos) $7.95

LITTLE BLUES CONCERTO
FOR 2 PIANOS, 4 HANDS
Early Intermediate Level
00142801 Piano Duo (2 Pianos, 4 Hands)........$12.99

TOUR FOR TWO
Late Elementary Level
00296832 6 Duets...............................$7.99

TREASURES
Late Elementary/Early Intermediate Level
00296924 7 Solos...............................$8.99

JEREMY SISKIND

BIG APPLE JAZZ
Intermediate Level
00278209 8 Solos...............................$8.99

MYTHS AND MONSTERS
Late Elementary/Early Intermediate Level
00148148 9 Solos...............................$7.99

CHRISTOS TSITSAROS

DANCES FROM AROUND THE WORLD
Early Intermediate Level
00296688 7 Solos...............................$8.99

LYRIC BALLADS
Intermediate/Late Intermediate Level
00102404 6 Solos...............................$8.99

POETIC MOMENTS
Intermediate Level
00296403 8 Solos...............................$8.99

SEA DIARY
Early Intermediate Level
00253486 9 Solos...............................$8.99

SONATINA HUMORESQUE
Late Intermediate Level
00296772 3 Movements $6.99

SONGS WITHOUT WORDS
Intermediate Level
00296506 9 Solos...............................$9.99

THREE PRELUDES
Early Advanced Level
00130747 ....$8.99

THROUGHOUT THE YEAR
Late Elementary Level
00296723 12 Duets.............................$6.95

ADDITIONAL COLLECTIONS

AT THE LAKE
by Elvina Pearce
Elementary/Late Elementary Level
00131642 10 Solos and Duets.....................$7.99

COUNTY RAGTIME FESTIVAL
by Fred Kern
Intermediate Level
00296882 7 Rags...............................$7.99

LITTLE JAZZERS
by Jennifer Watts
Elementary/Late Elementary Level
00154573 Solos.................................8.99

PLAY THE BLUES!
by Luann Carman (Method Book)
Early Intermediate Level
00296357 10 Solos.............................$9.99

Prices, contents, and availability subject
to change without notice.

HAL·LEONARD®
www.halleonard.com

Piano Recital Showcase

"What should my students play for the recital?" This series provides easy answers to this common question. For these winning collections, we've carefully selected some of the most popular and effective pieces from the **Hal Leonard Student Library** – from early-elementary to late-intermediate levels. You'll love the variety of musical styles found in each book.

PIANO RECITAL SHOWCASE PRE-STAFF

Pre-Staff Early Elementary Level
8 solos: Bumper Cars • Cherokee Lullaby • Fire Dance • The Hungry Spider • On a Magic Carpet • One, Two, Three • Pickled Pepper Polka • Pumpkin Song.
00296784 ....$7.99

BOOK 1

Elementary Level
12 solos: B.B.'s Boogie • In My Dreams • Japanese Garden • Jazz Jig • Joyful Bells • Lost Treasure • Monster March • Ocean Breezes • Party Cat Parade • Rainy Day Play • Sledding Fun • Veggie Song.
00296749 ....$8.99

BOOK 2

Late-Elementary Level
12 solos: Angelfish Arabesque • The Brontosaurus Bop • From the Land of Make-Believe • Ghosts of a Sunken Pirate Ship • The Happy Walrus • Harvest Dance • Hummingbird (L'oiseau-mouche) • Little Bird • Quick Spin in a Fast Car • Shifty-Eyed Blues • The Snake Charmer • Soft Shoe Shuffle.
00296748 ....$8.99

BOOK 3

Intermediate Level
10 solos: Castilian Dreamer • Dreaming Song • Jump Around Rag • Little Mazurka • Meaghan's Melody • Mountain Splendor • Seaside Stride • Snap to It! • Too Cool to Fool • Wizard's Wish.
00296747 ....$8.99

BOOK 4

Late-Intermediate Level
8 solos: Berceuse for Janey • Cafe Waltz • Forever in My Heart • Indigo Bay • Salsa Picante • Sassy Samba • Skater's Dream • Twilight on the Lake.
00296746 ....$8.99

CHRISTMAS EVE SOLOS

Intermediate Level
Composed for the intermediate level student, these pieces provide fresh and substantial repertoire for students not quite ready for advanced piano literature. Includes: Auld Lang Syne • Bring a Torch, Jeannette, Isabella • Coventry Carol • O Little Town of Bethlehem • Silent Night • We Wish You a Merry Christmas • and more.
00296877..$8.99

DUET FAVORITES

Intermediate Level
Five original duets for one piano, four hands from top composers Phillip Keveren, Eugénie Rocherolle, Sondra Clark and Wendy Stevens. Includes: Angel Falls • Crescent City Connection • Prime Time • A Wind of Promise • Yearning.
00296898..$9.99

FESTIVAL FAVORITES, BOOK 1
10 OUTSTANDING NFMC SELECTED SOLOS

Late Elementary/Early Intermediate Level
Proven piano solos fill this compilation of selected gems chosen for various National Federation of Music Clubs (NFMC) Junior Festival lists. Titles: Candlelight Prelude • Crazy Man's Blues • I've Gotta Toccata • Pagoda Bells • Tarantella • Toccata Festivo • Tonnerre sur les plaines (Thunder on the Plains) • Twister • Way Cool! • Wild Robot.
00118198..$10.99

FESTIVAL FAVORITES, BOOK 2
10 OUTSTANDING NFMC SELECTED SOLOS

Intermediate/Late Intermediate Level
Book 2 features: Barcarolle Impromptu • Cathedral Echoes (Harp Song) • Dance of the Trolls • Jasmine in the Mist • Jesters • Maestro, There's a Fly in My Waltz • Mother Earth, Sister Moon • Northwoods Toccata • Sounds of the Rain • Un phare dans le brouillard (A Lighthouse in the Fog).
00118202..$10.99

FESTIVAL GEMS – BOOK 1

Elementary/Late Elementary Level
This convenient collection features 10 NFMC-selected piano solos: Brooklyn's Waltz • Chimichanga Cha-Cha • Feelin' Happy • Footprints in the Snow • Lazy Daisy • New Orleans Jamboree • PBJ Blues • Pepperoni Pizza • Sneakin' Cake • Things That Go Bump in the Night. (Note: Solos are from previous NFMC lists.)
00193548 ....$10.99

HAL•LEONARD®

Visit our website at
www.halleonard.com/hlspl
for all the newest titles in this series and other books in the Hal Leonard Student Piano Library.

FESTIVAL GEMS – BOOK 2

Early Intermediate/Intermediate Level
Book 2 includes: Caravan • Chatterbox • In the Groove • Jubilation! • Kokopelli (Invention in Phrygian Mode) • La marée de soir (Evening Tide) • Reverie • Time Travel • Voiliers dans le vent (Sailboats in the Wind) • Williwaw.
00193587 ....$10.99

FESTIVAL GEMS – BOOK 3

Late Intermediate/Early Advanced Level
8 more NFMC-selected piano solos, including: Cuentos Del Matador (Tales of the Matador) • Daffodil Caprice • Love Song in the Rain • Midnight Prayer • Nocturne d'Esprit • Rapsodie • Scherzo • Urban Heartbeat.
00193588 ....$10.99

RAGTIME!

Early Intermediate/Intermediate Level
8 original rags from Bill Boyd, Phillip Keveren, Carol Klose, Jennifer Linn, Mona Rejino, Christos Tsitsaros and Jennifer & Mike Watts are featured in this solo piano collection. Includes: Butterfly Rag • Carnival Rag • Jump Around Rag • Nashville Rag • Ragtime Blue • St. Louis Rag • Swingin' Rag • Techno Rag.
00124242 ....$9.99

ROMANTIC INSPIRATIONS

Early Advanced Level
From "Arabesque" to "Nocturne" to "Rapsodie," the inspired pieces in this collection are a perfect choice for students who want to play beautiful, expressive and impressive literature at the recital. Includes: Arabesque • Journey's End • Nocturne • Nocturne d'Esprit • Prelude No. 1 • Rapsodie • Rondo Capriccioso • Valse d'Automne.
00296813..$8.99

SUMMERTIME FUN

Elementary Level
Twelve terrific originals from favorite HLSPL composers, all at the elementary level. Songs: Accidental Wizard • Butterflies and Rainbows • Chill Out! • Down by the Lake • The Enchanted Mermaid • Gone Fishin' • The Merry Merry-Go-Round • Missing You • Pink Lemonade • Rockin' the Boat • Teeter-Totter • Wind Chimes.
00296831 ....$7.99

COMPOSER SHOWCASE
HAL LEONARD STUDENT PIANO LIBRARY

This series showcases great original piano music from our **Hal Leonard Student Piano Library** family of composers. Carefully graded for easy selection.

BILL BOYD

JAZZ BITS (AND PIECES)
Early Intermediate Level
00290312 11 Solos......................$7.99

JAZZ DELIGHTS
Intermediate Level
00240435 11 Solos......................$8.99

JAZZ FEST
Intermediate Level
00240436 10 Solos......................$8.99

JAZZ PRELIMS
Early Elementary Level
00290032 12 Solos......................$7.99

JAZZ SKETCHES
Intermediate Level
00220001 8 Solos......................$8.99

JAZZ STARTERS
Elementary Level
00290425 10 Solos......................$8.99

JAZZ STARTERS II
Late Elementary Level
00290434 11 Solos......................$7.99

JAZZ STARTERS III
Late Elementary Level
00290465 12 Solos......................$8.99

THINK JAZZ!
Early Intermediate Level
00290417 Method Book............$12.99

TONY CARAMIA

JAZZ MOODS
Intermediate Level
00296728 8 Solos......................$6.95

SUITE DREAMS
Intermediate Level
00296775 4 Solos......................$6.99

SONDRA CLARK

DAKOTA DAYS
Intermediate Level
00296521 5 Solos......................$6.95

FLORIDA FANTASY SUITE
Intermediate Level
00296766 3 Duets......................$7.95

THREE ODD METERS
Intermediate Level
00296472 3 Duets......................$6.95

MATTHEW EDWARDS

CONCERTO FOR YOUNG PIANISTS
FOR 2 PIANOS, FOUR HANDS
Intermediate Level Book/CD
00296356 3 Movements $19.99

CONCERTO NO. 2 IN G MAJOR
FOR 2 PIANOS, 4 HANDS
Intermediate Level Book/CD
00296670 3 Movements............$17.99

PHILLIP KEVEREN

MOUSE ON A MIRROR
Late Elementary Level
00296361 5 Solos......................$8.99

MUSICAL MOODS
Elementary/Late Elementary Level
00296714 7 Solos......................$6.99

SHIFTY-EYED BLUES
Late Elementary Level
00296374 5 Solos......................$7.99

CAROL KLOSE

THE BEST OF CAROL KLOSE
Early to Late Intermediate Level
00146151 15 Solos....................$12.99

CORAL REEF SUITE
Late Elementary Level
00296354 7 Solos......................$7.50

DESERT SUITE
Intermediate Level
00296667 6 Solos......................$7.99

FANCIFUL WALTZES
Early Intermediate Level
00296473 5 Solos......................$7.95

GARDEN TREASURES
Late Intermediate Level
00296787 5 Solos......................$8.50

ROMANTIC EXPRESSIONS
Intermediate to Late Intermediate Level
00296923 5 Solos......................$8.99

WATERCOLOR MINIATURES
Early Intermediate Level
00296848 7 Solos......................$7.99

JENNIFER LINN

AMERICAN IMPRESSIONS
Intermediate Level
00296471 6 Solos......................$8.99

ANIMALS HAVE FEELINGS TOO
Early Elementary/Elementary Level
00147789 8 Solos......................$8.99

AU CHOCOLAT
Late Elementary/Early Intermediate Level
00298110 7 Solos......................$8.99

CHRISTMAS IMPRESSIONS
Intermediate Level
00296706 8 Solos......................$8.99

JUST PINK
Elementary Level
00296722 9 Solos......................$8.99

LES PETITES IMAGES
Late Elementary Level
00296664 7 Solos......................$8.99

LES PETITES IMPRESSIONS
Intermediate Level
00296355 6 Solos......................$8.99

REFLECTIONS
Late Intermediate Level
00296843 5 Solos......................$8.99

TALES OF MYSTERY
Intermediate Level
00296769 6 Solos......................$8.99

LYNDA LYBECK-ROBINSON

ALASKA SKETCHES
Early Intermediate Level
00119637 8 Solos......................$8.99

AN AWESOME ADVENTURE
Late Elementary Level
00137563 8 Solos......................$7.99

FOR THE BIRDS
Early Intermediate/Intermediate Level
00237078 9 Solos......................$8.99

WHISPERING WOODS
Late Elementary Level
00275905 9 Solos......................$8.99

MONA REJINO

CIRCUS SUITE
Late Elementary Level
00296665 5 Solos......................$8.99

COLOR WHEEL
Early Intermediate Level
00201951 6 Solos......................$9.99

IMPRESIONES DE ESPAÑA
Intermediate Level
00337520 6 Solos......................$8.99

IMPRESSIONS OF NEW YORK
Intermediate Level
00364212.................................$8.99

JUST FOR KIDS
Elementary Level
00296840 8 Solos......................$7.99

MERRY CHRISTMAS MEDLEYS
Intermediate Level
00296799 5 Solos......................$8.99

MINIATURES IN STYLE
Intermediate Level
00148088 6 Solos......................$8.99

PORTRAITS IN STYLE
Early Intermediate Level
00296507 6 Solos......................$8.99

EUGÉNIE ROCHEROLLE

CELEBRATION SUITE
Intermediate Level
00152724 3 Duets......................$8.99

ENCANTOS ESPAÑOLES (SPANISH DELIGHTS)
Intermediate Level
00125451 6 Solos......................$8.99

JAMBALAYA
Intermediate Level
00296654 2 Pianos, 8 Hands.....$12.99
00296725 2 Pianos, 4 Hands.......$7.95

JEROME KERN CLASSICS
Intermediate Level
00296577 10 Solos....................$12.99

LITTLE BLUES CONCERTO
Early Intermediate Level
00142801 2 Pianos, 4 Hands......$12.99

TOUR FOR TWO
Late Elementary Level
00296832 6 Duets......................$9.99

TREASURES
Late Elementary/Early Intermediate Level
00296924 7 Solos......................$8.99

JEREMY SISKIND

BIG APPLE JAZZ
Intermediate Level
00278209 8 Solos......................$8.99

MYTHS AND MONSTERS
Late Elementary/Early Intermediate Level
00148148 9 Solos......................$8.99

CHRISTOS TSITSAROS

DANCES FROM AROUND THE WORLD
Early Intermediate Level
00296688 7 Solos......................$8.99

FIVE SUMMER PIECES
Late Intermediate/Advanced Level
00361235 5 Solos....................$12.99

LYRIC BALLADS
Intermediate/Late Intermediate Level
00102404 6 Solos......................$8.99

POETIC MOMENTS
Intermediate Level
00296403 8 Solos......................$8.99

SEA DIARY
Early Intermediate Level
00253486 9 Solos......................$8.99

SONATINA HUMORESQUE
Late Intermediate Level
00296772 3 Movements..............$6.99

SONGS WITHOUT WORDS
Intermediate Level
00296506 9 Solos......................$9.99

THREE PRELUDES
Early Advanced Level
00130747 3 Solos......................$8.99

THROUGHOUT THE YEAR
Late Elementary Level
00296723 12 Duets....................$6.95

ADDITIONAL COLLECTIONS

AT THE LAKE
by Elvina Pearce
Elementary/Late Elementary Level
00131642 10 Solos and Duets.....$7.99

CHRISTMAS FOR TWO
by Dan Fox
Early Intermediate Level
00290069 13 Duets....................$8.99

CHRISTMAS JAZZ
by Mike Springer
Intermediate Level
00296525 6 Solos......................$8.99

COUNTY RAGTIME FESTIVAL
by Fred Kern
Intermediate Level
00296882 7 Solos......................$7.99

LITTLE JAZZERS
by Jennifer Watts
Elementary/Late Elementary Level
00154573 9 Solos......................$8.99

PLAY THE BLUES!
by Luann Carman
Early Intermediate Level
00296357 10 Solos....................$9.99

ROLLER COASTERS & RIDES
by Jennifer & Mike Watts
Intermediate Level
00131144 8 Duets......................$8.99

www.halleonard.com

Prices, contents, and availability subject to change without notice.

0321

144